Dogs

to paint or color

JOHN GREEN

DOVER PUBLICATIONS, INC.
MINEOLA, NEW YORK

Note

This delightful coloring book features a sampling of dogs and puppies that represent seven of the different breed groups. There are German shorthaired pointers out for a hunt, a flat-coated retriever playing catch, an Australian shepherd watching the flock, a proud golden retriever with her pups, and nineteen other dogs included in this beautifully detailed collection of canines. Some of the dogs are pictured working and hunting in a natural setting and others are shown as companions at home.

Watch the printed lines practically disappear as you create your own personal masterpieces using pencil, pen, paint, or any other media. The illustrations are printed on one side only on high-quality paper making them suitable for framing when completed. To remove the pages, carefully tear them out following the perforation.

Copyright

Copyright © 2008 by Dover Publications, Inc.
All rights reserved.

Bibliographical Note

Dogs to Paint or Color is a new work, first published by Dover Publications, Inc., in 2008.

International Standard Book Number

ISBN-13: 978-0-486-46541-8
ISBN-10: 0-486-46541-1

Manufactured in the United States by Courier Corporation
46541104   2014
www.doverpublications.com

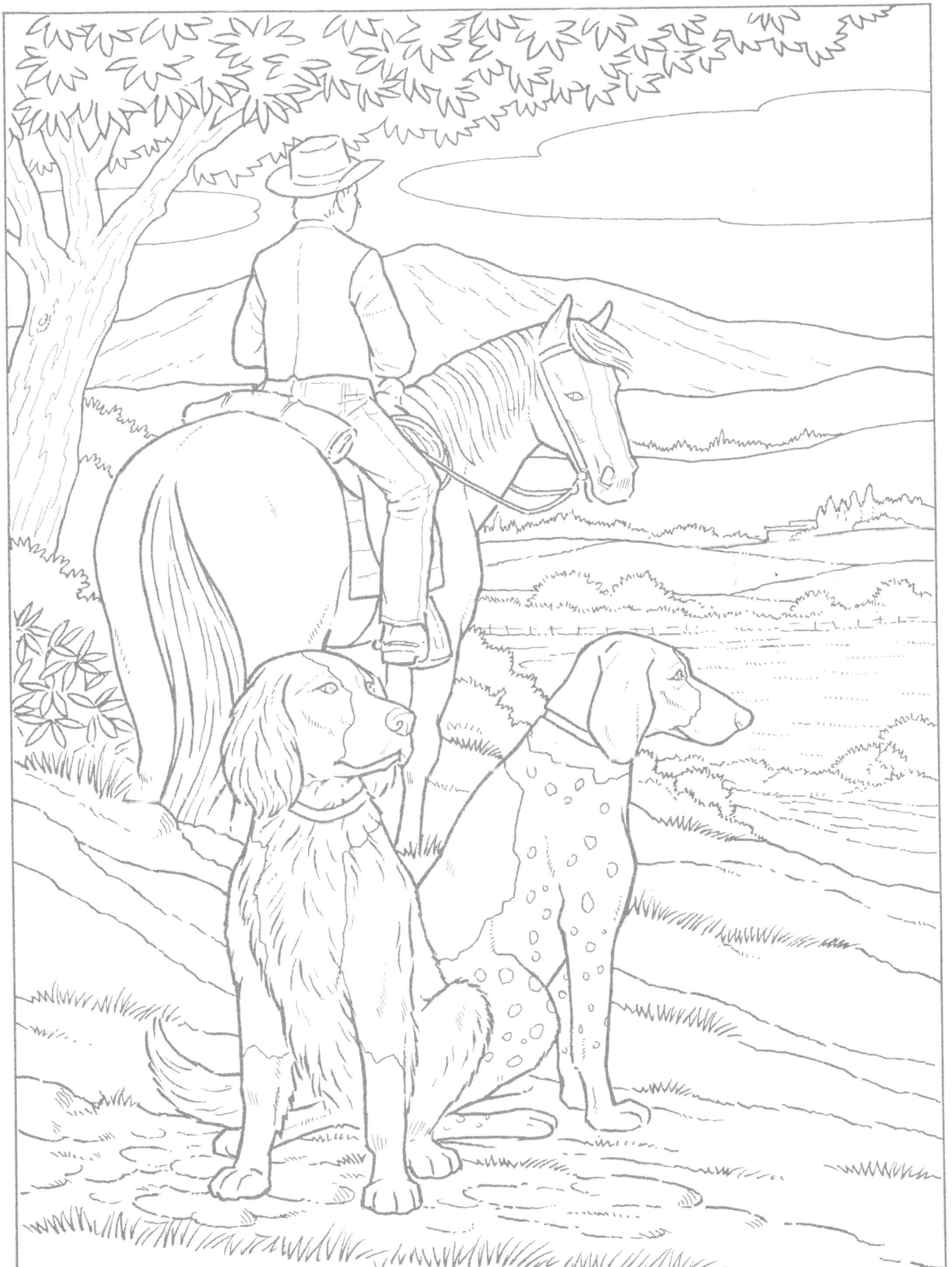

German Longhaired Pointer / German Shorthaired Pointer

we can't ~~talk.~~ talk.

If you are done first you have to wait for me to me to

Still we don't know
when to talk
when we are done coloring,

ok!

Haha
Ha ok
ok when
were
done

we have to keep it going else ok!
it want be a talking challenge, then we can

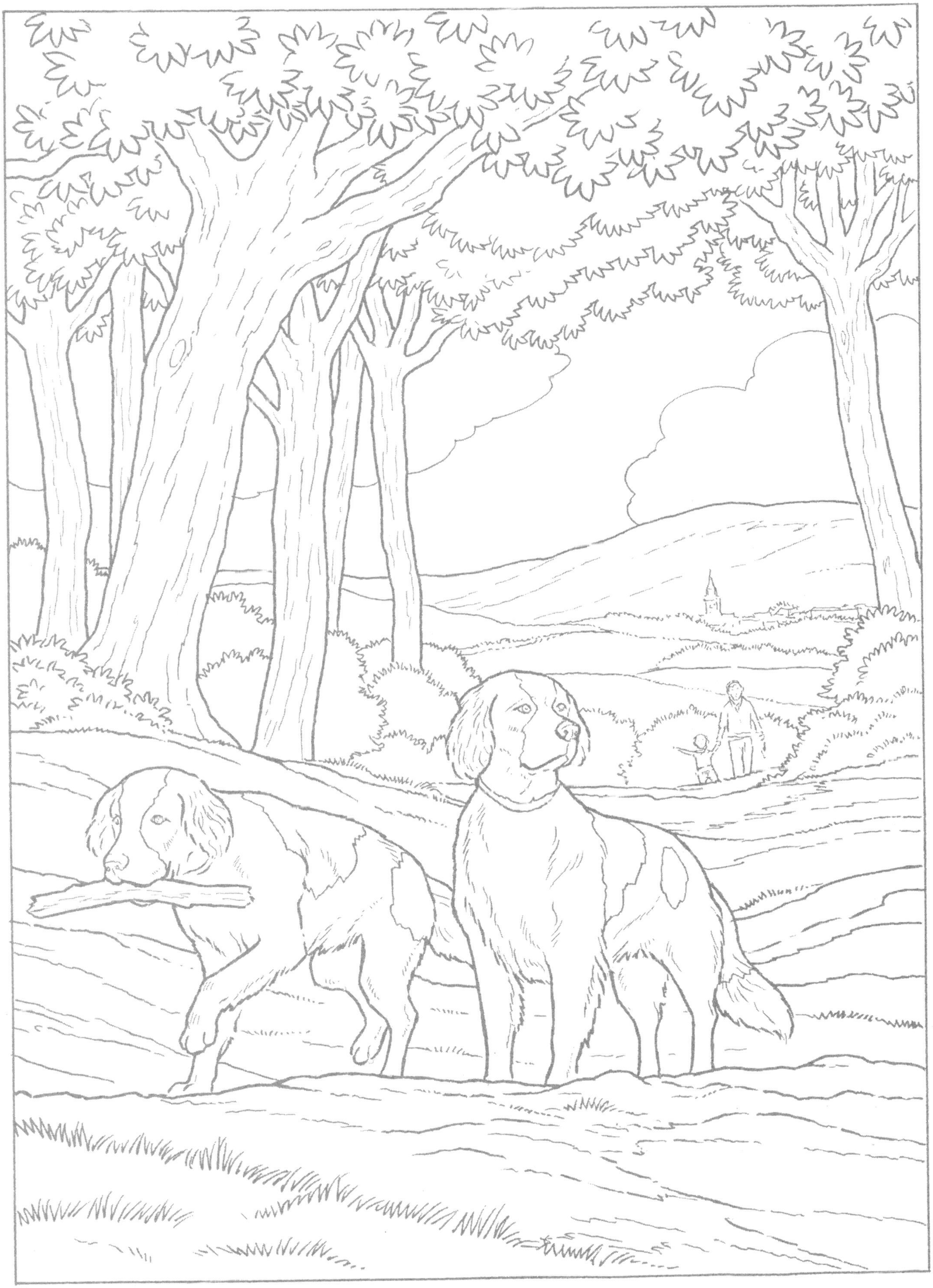

English Setters

Greyhounds